SCIENCE OF SPORTS

THE SCIENCE OF BASKETBALL

WITH MAX AXIOM SUPER SCIENTIST

by Nikole Brooks Bethea

illustrated by Maurizio Campidelli

Consultant:
Lyle A. Ford
Department Chair
Physics & Astronomy
University of Wisconsin, Eau Claire

CAPSTONE PRESS
a capstone imprint

Graphic Library is published by Capstone Press,
1710 Roe Crest Drive, North Mankato, Minnesota 56003
www.capstonepub.com

Library of Congress Cataloging-in-Publication Data
Bethea, Nikole Brooks.
The science of basketball with Max Axiom, super scientist / by Nikole B. Bethea.
     pages cm. — (Graphic Library. The Science of Sports with Max Axiom.)
Includes bibliographical references and index.
Summary: "Uses graphic novel format to reveal the scientific aspects at play in the sport of
basketball"— Provided by publisher.
  ISBN 978-1-4914-6084-9 (library binding)
  ISBN 978-1-4914-6088-7 (paperback)
  ISBN 978-1-4914-6092-4 (eBook PDF)
  1. Basketball—Juvenile literature. 2. Sports sciences—Juvenile literature. 3. Graphic novels—
Juvenile literature. I. Title.
  GV885.1.B47 2016
  796.323—dc23   2015012515

Editor
Mandy Robbins

Designer
Ted Williams

Creative Director
Nathan Gassman

Cover Artist
Caio Cacau

Media Researcher
Jo Miller

Production Specialist
Laura Manthe

Printed and bound in the United States of America.
002073

TABLE OF CONTENTS

Now we're going to switch over from the running part of the game to shooting. The angle of a shot is important, which is easily demonstrated when shooting a free throw.

The trajectory of the ball is the path it takes from your hand to the basket. The shape of the trajectory is a parabola.

Let's use my stop-motion glasses to go back in time a few seconds. We see the ball at the top of its trajectory. It reaches a maximum height. Then gravity pulls it down.

The ball doesn't usually drop straight down into the basket. The arched trajectory causes it to go in at an angle.

Different approach angles cause the rim to "change shape."

The shot with a 70° approach angle was the easiest to make. Now it makes sense why it works that way!

30°

9 inches

50°

16 inches

70°

17-25 inches

The 30° entry is the hardest of the three shots to make. It's nearly a flat shot. The rim appears like a squished oval. But with a 70° shot, the rim appears nearly circular.

11

Wow! What is that? Where did it come from?

This is Sir Isaac Newton. I brought him here from the 1600s in my time machine. In 1687 he published three Laws of Motion.

My First Law is: An object at rest stays at rest. An object in motion stays in motion, unless a force acts on it.

A force is a push or a pull. I remember that from science class.

My First Law is also called the Law of Inertia. Inertia is the tendency of an object to resist a change in motion.

So, when I'm running, the basketball's inertia has forward motion. It keeps moving forward with my body.

In the 1600s Galileo dropped objects from the mast of a moving ship. From his perspective, the objects fell straight down. They landed at the bottom of the mast. Some people might have assumed the objects would have fallen behind the mast since the ship moved forward. However, the objects moved forward at the same speed as the ship. They had inertia.

Jumping is an important skill in basketball. I'm sure Mr. Newton can explain what makes jumping possible. Isaac?

My Third Law says that when one object exerts a force on another object, the second object exerts an equal and opposite force on the first.

Is that the same law that says that for every action there is an equal and opposite reaction?

You got it!

When you start to jump, your feet push down on the floor.

The floor is connected to the building, which is anchored to the ground. This combination has a huge mass. Your small push doesn't move the floor any noticeable distance.

GYMNASIUM

Wow, Max. I can't believe you know Brooks Lee! And that Newton guy and his laws? That's incredible!

There is one scientific law we didn't go over: the Law of Conservation of Energy.

Dribbling the basketball demonstrates the Law of Conservation of Energy. This law states that energy cannot be created or destroyed, but it can be changed from one form into another.

What do you mean by energy?

Energy is the ability to do work. And believe it or not, there's more than one kind.

Funny enough, we're exhibiting it right now.

By practicing your bounce pass with both a fully inflated basketball and a slightly flat basketball, you can learn about air pressure.

I notice that the flat ball doesn't bounce as high.

I've frozen time to when the balls bounced off the court, and I've shrunk us down to get a closer look at them. What do you notice?

The inflated ball has a much smaller deformation where it hits the ground than the flat ball. The flat ball looks like it's been punched.

Whoa! Ouch! Max where are we? What's going on here?

I've shrunk us down to molecular size and put us inside the fully inflated ball so you could see what goes on inside it.

All of those items smacking us around are air molecules. The well-inflated basketball has more air molecules inside. The less-inflated ball has fewer air molecules. These tiny particles of air are made up of atoms. What do you think about that?

I think you should have transported us into the flat ball. YOUCH!

Point taken. Let's get out of here and back to regular size.

Okay, now look. Both basketballs get squished when they collide with the floor.

The collision squeezes and pushes the air molecules inside the balls.

The molecules collide with each other and the inside surface of the ball.

Pressure is the force over an area. Since more molecules are in the well-inflated ball, there are more collisions with the basketball's inside surface than in the flat ball. More collisions mean more force is applied to the inside area of the ball.

That means the air pressure inside the well-inflated ball is greater.

That's right! And that's why the well-inflated ball bounces higher.

As a gas is heated, its molecules move faster. They bump into each other and spread out. The gas expands. As a gas is cooled, its molecules move slower. The gas contracts. This is why a helium balloon kept inside a cool house seems to blow up when it is taken outside.

Wow! That's a hard pass!

By understanding Newton's Second Law of motion, you can lessen the impact of a chest pass.

This law tells us that the force of an object is equal to its mass times its acceleration. This is often stated as F = M * A.

The basketball has momentum when I pass it to you. Momentum is mass times velocity. It is basically mass in motion.

MOMENTUM = MASS x VELOCITY

If you remember that acceleration is the change in velocity over time, you can rewrite Newton's Second Law as F = M * V/T.

Since mass times velocity is momentum, force is the change in momentum over time.

$$F = M \times A$$
$$A = V/T$$
$$F = M \times V/T$$

Who knew basketball involved this much math?

When we write the equation as F = M * V/T, we see that dividing by a larger time will make the force less. By bending your arms and bringing the basketball toward you, the time to catch the ball increases.

$$F = M \times V/T$$

Increasing the amount of time to catch the pass makes the impact of the pass less. The pass is easier to catch.

No problem!

By the way, speaking of passing, all this studying has me feeling great about passing my science test.

With your new knowledge of science, I bet your basketball game will improve too!

MORE ABOUT BASKETBALL

James Naismith invented the game of basketball in 1891. He was searching for a game that the YMCA could play indoors during Massachusetts' cold winters. The original game was played using a soccer ball with two peach baskets as goals.

Basketball became an official Olympic event in 1936 at the Games in Berlin, Germany.

Both the National Basketball Association (NBA) and the Women's National Basketball Association (WNBA) require basketballs to have a pressure between 7.5 and 8.5 pounds (3.4 to 3.8 kilograms) per square inch.

A warm basketball is bouncier than a cold basketball. This is partly because molecules move faster at higher temperatures. The molecules in the warm ball hit the inside surface of the ball at a higher speed.

Physics professor Dr. Gintaras Duda of Creighton University has determined what makes a perfect three-point shot. It would be shot from 20.9 feet (6.4 m) from the basket with an arc of 45 degrees. Its speed would be just under 20 miles (32 kilometers) per hour, and it would spin two revolutions per second.

Shooting free throws underhand is actually more accurate than the typical shooting style. This type of shot is often called a "granny shot." Hall of Fame NBA player Rick Barry was the only professional to ever shoot his free throws granny-style. His shot them with 90-percent accuracy.

Basketball players don't wear a lot of gear, but the one piece of equipment they have that can affect their game is their shoes. However, a study from the British Journal of Sports Medicine found that expensive "air cell" sneakers can actually cause more ankle injuries to basketball players than other shoes.

 When shooting a basketball, a wrist snap happens in just one-tenth of a second.

 A 3-foot (0.9-m) vertical jump has a hang time of 0.87 second, while a 4-foot (1.2-m) vertical jump has a hang time of 1 second.

MORE ABOUT

SUPER SCIENTIST

Real name: Maxwell J. Axiom
Hometown: Seattle, Washington
Height: 6' 1"   Weight: 192 lbs
Eyes: Brown   Hair: None

Super capabilities: Super intelligence; able to shrink to the size of an atom; sunglasses give X-ray vision; lab coat allows for travel through time and space.

Origin: Since birth, Max Axiom seemed destined for greatness. His mother, a marine biologist, taught her son about the mysteries of the sea. His father, a nuclear physicist and volunteer park ranger, schooled Max on the wonders of earth and sky.

One day on a wilderness hike, a megacharged lightning bolt struck Max with blinding fury. When he awoke, Max discovered a newfound energy and set out to learn as much about science as possible. He traveled the globe earning degrees in every aspect of the field. Upon his return, he was ready to share his knowledge and new identity with the world. He had become Max Axiom, Super Scientist.

GLOSSARY

acceleration (ak-sel-uh-RAY-shuhn)—the change in speed of a moving body

contract (kuhn-TRAKT)—to tighten and get shorter by squeezing in toward the middle

energy (EN-ur-jee)—the ability to do work

force (FORS)—any action that changes the movement of an object

friction (FRIK-shuhn)—a force produced when two objects rub against each other; friction slows down objects

hang time (HANG TYME)—the amount of time the ball or ball player spends in the air

inertia (in-UR-shuh)—the tendency of an object to remain either at rest or in motion unless affected by an outside force

kinetic energy (ki-NET-ik EN-ur-jee)—the energy of a moving object

mass (MASS)—the amount of material in an object

molecule (MOL-uh-kyool)—the smallest part of an element that can exist and still keep the characteristics of the element

momentum (moh-MEN-tuhm)—the force or speed created by movement

potential energy (puh-TEN-shuhl EN-ur-jee)—energy stored within an object, waiting to be released

pressure (PRESH-ur)—the force produced by pressing on something

trajectory (truh-JEK-tuh-ree)—the path an object takes as it moves

velocity (vuh-LOSS-uh-tee)—a measurement of both the speed and direction an object is moving

READ MORE

Adamson, Thomas K. *Basketball: The Math of the Game.* Mankato, Minn: Capstone Press, 2012.

Amazing Sports and Science. Time for Kids Book of Why. New York: Time for Kids Books, 2014.

McKerley, Jennifer Guess. *Football.* Science Behind Sports. Detroit: Lucent Books, 2012.

Slade, Suzanne. *Basketball: How It Works.* The Science of Sports. Mankato, Minn: Capstone Press, 2010.

Yancey, Diane. *Basketball.* Detroit: Lucent Books, 2011.

INTERNET SITES

FactHound offers a safe, fun way to find Internet sites related to this book. All sites on FactHound have been researched by our staff.

Here's all you do:

Visit *www.facthound.com*

Type in this code: 9781491460849

Check out projects, games and lots more at
www.capstonekids.com

INDEX